An Unlikely Bartender
Crafting a New Legacy in Cocktails

ISBN: 979-8-218-31741-6

Cover photo by Christopher Hwang

Photos by Christopher Hwang: Pages 20, 22, 24, 26, 28, 30, 32, 34, 36, 38, 40, 42, 44, 46, 48, 50, 54, 56, 60, 62, 64, 66, 68, 72, 76, 78, 80, 84, 86, 88

Photos by Erica Everhart: Pages: 4, 15, 74

Photos by Deb Lindsey: Pages: 18, 52, 82

Photo by Aleksandre Sandro: Page 70

Photo by Getty Images (2019): Page 140

First Edition

For Ruth, Sam, Sarah, and Simon

I extend my heartfelt gratitude to everyone who worked at the bar, in the kitchen, and on the floor. Your collective efforts elevated the experience and fostered a vibrant and collaborative environment. Thank you for being an integral part of this remarkable process.

To Ruth, Hugo, Sara, Brian, Vicky, Mark, and Ilana for taking the journey.

An Unlikely Bartender

Crafting a New Legacy in Cocktails

Michael Biddick

CONTENTS

PART I

INTRODUCTION

WELCOME

I don't know much about cocktails. My expertise lies in information technology (IT), where I have dedicated my professional career to consulting with large enterprise organizations to help them address their most challenging technological and leadership issues. After almost 20 years in consulting, despite having no experience in restaurants or bartending, I embarked on an adventure to open Blend 111, a 45 seat restaurant in Vienna, Virginia. This inaugural voyage of mine, filled with its share of stumbles and learning curves, produced a collection of unique cocktails that our guests constantly enjoyed even as we evolved our menu and service.

While presenting its unique challenges, my lack of traditional experience also left me unshackled by the conventional wisdom of the cocktail canon. I saw cocktails, like the intricate systems that I was accustomed to in the digital world, as complex, layered stories. They presented an opportunity to weave a rich tapestry of culture with strands of herbs, fruits, spirits, and spices. Even without formal training in mixology, I had a keen sense of what tasted good and possessed the ability to refine drinks based on immediate feedback.

As an IT consultant turned cocktail connoisseur and back again, this book chronicles my excursion into the world of mixology. It captures the rich insights and experiences gained during my tenure at Blend 111's bar, a period that was not just a detour from technology, but a valuable journey of learning and growth in the art of crafting cocktails. Here, you might miss the bedrock principles of classic mixology and point out gaps and inconsistencies. Still, you may also discover some innovative concoctions born of my experimentation and novice approach. Whether you're an amateur mixer or a spirit savant, these recipes offer my efforts to balance the time-honored and the contemporary.

Within these pages lies an invitation to peer over the shoulder of an IT consultant turned mixologist, where respect for tradition dovetails with the practicalities of running a small restaurant. Balancing the avoidance of time-consuming preparations and grandstanding presentations with a focus on quality ingredients and consistent execution was the goal.

In these cocktails, I sought an elegance in simplicity. I tried to maximize flavor and minimize fuss. My mantra: pare down to amplify, distill the essence, eschew the artificial, and banish the over-processed. Here, in the uncluttered space where flavors bloom, we find our true north—crafting simple drinks that speak volumes through their understated complexity.

Approach this collection like new software—a base code to be enhanced, refined, and debugged with flair. To the patrons of Blend 111, the memories encoded within its walls, and the enthusiasts of tomorrow, this volume is a tribute to our cocktails. Here's to the past, the present, and the yet-to-be-discovered possibilities.

My aspiration for writing this book is to encourage exploring new endeavors and embracing risk and innovation. Expect the unexpected and recognize that some attempts may not unfold as planned. In fact, you might have failures. What's crucial is gaining insight from each endeavor, especially the failures, and always moving forward.

Michael Biddick

ROAD TO THE BAR

I spent my childhood in a sleepy suburban area outside Milwaukee during the 1980s. Life there was quiet, and my encounters with alcohol were sparse. For me, fun was playing with Star Wars action figures, wandering around the neighborhood with friends, or visiting my grandparents across town. My parents weren't big drinkers, usually opting for a nondescript glass of wine or the occasional beer. We just didn't talk or even think a lot about booze.

As I progressed through high school, some of my peers started to dabble in the beer scene. But that world remained mostly on the periphery for me. College in Madison didn't change much despite the city's buzzing party reputation. My brushes with alcohol there were sporadic—a spiked punch bowl here, a rare bar visit there, usually where the bouncers weren't too strict.

During the late 1990s, I moved to Washington, DC, where the nightlife buzzed with dance clubs and bars, albeit with basic cocktail menus. The food and bar scene in the late 1990s and early 2000s was not what it is today. You could go blocks and not even find a restaurant or a bar, especially one worth stopping in to try. My cocktail game, like the city's food scene, was unimpressive.

Professionally, though, my focus was elsewhere. After arriving in Washington, I became part of a global consulting firm tackling projects for various government and private sector clients. It was the heyday of the dot-com boom, and my attention was on honing enterprise network management solutions.

As the new millennium rolled in, I started traveling across Europe and South and Central America. These trips exposed me to a world of wine and cocktails I'd never known. I delved into a kaleidoscope of new flavors, each sip and swirl teaching me a bit about the craft and culture of cocktails.

By the end of the '90s, I had shifted to a smaller consulting firm, working my way up to an executive role. In 2009, my wife Ruth and I embarked on a new venture, founding Fusion PPT. Our IT consulting firm was at the forefront of emerging tech fields, specializing in cloud computing, cybersecurity, and the early stages of artificial intelligence development.

The growing frequency of personal and business travel, along with dining experiences, fueled a parallel interest in wine, a complex subject that I found as fascinating as the world of IT. My journey became one of education, of visiting vineyards, chatting with experts, and soaking in all I could about the intricate world of wine. My serious study of wine kicked off in 2017. I engaged with the Court of Master Sommeliers, going through the "Certified" exam, and completed the Wine Scholar Guild program on French wine, becoming a Master of Bordeaux Wines. This foundation was supplemented by recreational trips to the viniculture heartlands of Spain and France, enriching my understanding and appreciation of wine's cultural significance.

Then came 2018, a landmark year when Fusion PPT was acquired, and I found myself up against a non-compete agreement. IT consulting was off the table for three years. Far from considering retirement, I embraced this juncture to delve into a new venture—a wine bar. However, Virginia's liquor laws required that we serve food if we wanted to pour drinks. At the time, I didn't appreciate the complexity and costs of transforming this vision into an upscale restaurant. Collaborating with neighbors, we created Blend 111, a mix of bar and restaurant that opened in May 2019.

Those early days were filled with steep learning curves and a revolving door of staff. Some of these missteps were meticulously documented in a *Washington Post* review shortly after we opened our doors. But we found our footing about 10 months after opening, only to be challenged by the pandemic. Forced to close for a time, we offered delivery services and curbside pickup with a new food and cocktail menu. I found myself working as a hands-on manager and bartender during those critical months, immersed in every aspect of the restaurant.

The pandemic's adversity brought unexpected opportunities. Our town permitted us to set up an outdoor patio, which quickly became our guests' cherished spot. I found a talented new chef and new front-of-house staff eager to devote their talents to our small establishment. This period brought us accolades and positive press, including recognition from *Northern Virginia Magazine* and favorable reviews from *Washington Post* critic Tom Sietsema. Our presence in local media, including radio and television, solidified our gastronomic reputation. These years were transformative, heralding what I think of as Blend 111's renaissance, the era in which we crafted cocktails that weren't just drinks but narratives in a glass, testaments to our journey and passion for quality, innovation, resilience, and hospitality.

Our wine-centered approach adapted to an emerging trend among our patrons: a growing love for cocktails. It became clear that the world was shifting; wine was giving way to a broadening interest in various spirits, mixed drinks, and zero-proof offerings. My growing appreciation for the complexities of mixology signified a pivotal pause from my career in IT consulting and led me to the journey of writing this book.

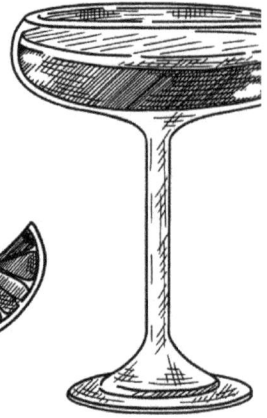

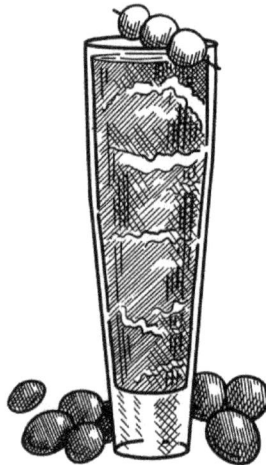

PART II

COCKTAILS

Alma

Alma means "soul" in Spanish; this drink was crafted to capture the essence of the ingredients, a blended dance of both Italian and Mexican flavors embodying a fusion of traditions and tastes with rich complexity—bitter, sweet, smoky, and sour notes all vie for attention, much like the different aspects of one's soul.

½ oz. amaro

½ oz. organic blue agave

2 oz. mezcal

½ oz. lemon juice

Add all ingredients to a shaker filled halfway with ice. Shake vigorously for about ten seconds. Strain the mixture into a glass. Garnish with a dehydrated blood orange wheel.

Avispas

Cocktails don't need to be complicated to be delicious. For example, the Avispas was the simplest cocktail that I created and, far and away, the most popular week after week. The magical ingredient is the bee pollen sprinkled on top, floating on the ice. The texture and the slightly sweet and grassy-floral tastes of the pollen make this drink absolutely delicious.

2 oz. bourbon

1 oz. organic blue agave

1 oz. lemon juice

Add all ingredients to a shaker filled halfway with ice. Shake vigorously for about ten seconds. Strain the mixture into a glass filled with fresh ice. For garnish, carefully sprinkle one teaspoon of bee pollen over the top of the ice.

Bajo el Puente Rafael Urdaneta

This cocktail encapsulates a spirited night I spent on a party boat under the iconic bridge in Maracaibo, Venezuela, during the early 2000s. Named after the Puente Rafael Urdaneta, this drink reflects the lively atmosphere as the city's rhythm resonated across the dark waters of Lake Maracaibo.

1 ½ oz. gin

¾ oz. lime juice

¾ oz. Aperol

1 oz. papaya purée (pages 99, 101)

¼ oz. organic blue agave

Add all ingredients to a shaker filled halfway with ice. Shake vigorously for about ten seconds. Strain into the glass and garnish by placing candied ginger on the rim.

Bordeaux Sour

In 2022, *Liquor Magazine* cast a spotlight upon our Bordeaux sour, elegantly positioning it within a curated selection of avant-garde interpretations of the venerable whisky sour. I had assembled an anthology of organic wines handpicked from the storied terroirs of Spain and France. The integration of these wines into our cocktail offerings was nothing short of alchemical.

2 oz. bourbon

2 premium maraschino cherries

1 oz. lemon juice

1 oz. organic red wine

¼ oz. sparkling water

1 oz. aquafaba (page 92)

½ oz. real maple syrup

5 dashes orange bitters

In a shaker, muddle the cherries with lemon juice and maple syrup. Add the remaining ingredients along with ice and shake well. Strain the mixture into the glass over fresh ice. Top with sparkling water and garnish with a maraschino cherry placed atop the ice—it may sink, but that's part of the charm.

Café Carisma

The Café Carisma is my take on the classic espresso martini, crafted not just as a beverage but as an experience. While the essence of freshly roasted coffee plays a role in its depth, here it complements rather than commands the spotlight, allowing the harmonious balance of flavors to enchant the palate.

1 ¼ oz. vodka

2 oz. espresso (page 96)

¼ oz. coffee liqueur

¾ oz. demerara syrup (page 97)

Add all ingredients to a shaker filled halfway with ice. Shake vigorously for about ten seconds. Strain the mixture into a glass. Garnish with three coffee beans.

Cali

This cocktail pays tribute to Cali's nightlife. The anise-flavored spirit embodies the fervor of Colombia's salsa capital with its rich cultural tapestry. As dancers sway to salsa rhythms, aguardiente fuels their zest, mirroring Cali's vibrant pulse. It's a celebration intertwining with the city's spirited soul.

2 oz. aguardiente

5 dashes bitters

2 oz. pink guava purée
(pages 99, 103)

¾ oz. lime juice

Add all ingredients to a shaker filled halfway with ice. Shake vigorously for about ten seconds. Strain the mixture into a glass filled with fresh ice. To garnish, add a sprig of fresh mint, sliding it against the inside of the glass.

Cerecita

This cocktail came to life a little over a year following the inception of the Bordeaux sour, bearing a semblance in the ingredient mix yet diverging with a distinct base spirit. The flavor narrative took a bold turn with a smoky mezcal heralding the dominant note, crafting a flavor profile that stood apart, embracing a character entirely its own.

1 ½ oz. tequila

½ oz. organic blue agave

½ oz. cherry liqueur

1 oz. organic red wine

½ oz. mezcal

¾ oz. lime juice

Add all ingredients to a shaker filled halfway with ice. Shake vigorously for about ten seconds. Strain the mixture into a salt-rimmed glass filled with fresh ice. Garnish by skewering a Luxardo cherry and a lime wheel on a bamboo stick and resting it on top of the drink.

Che

This cocktail channels the revolutionary spirit of Che Guevara, mixing singani with chile liqueur and pink guava for a drink that's as bold and complex as Che's journey—a tribute in a glass to the fire of change. It's a drink crafted not just to savor but to spark conversation and reflection on the indomitable will of one of history's most iconic revolutionaries.

1 ¼ oz. singani

¼ oz. demerara syrup

1 oz. chile liqueur

½ oz. pink guava purée
(pages 99, 103)

1 oz. lemon juice

Add all ingredients to a shaker filled halfway with ice. Shake vigorously for about ten seconds. Strain the mixture into a glass filled with fresh ice. Garnish with a chile-dusted lemon wheel.

Cienfuegos

Cienfuegos, located on the southern coast of Cuba, is celebrated for its French influences, colonial-era architecture, and picturesque bay. Here, French Chartreuse finds its way into this invigorating tropical beverage, lending an aura of charm to each sip.

2 oz. white rum

½ oz. organic blue agave

½ oz. yellow Chartreuse

¼ oz. passion fruit purée
(pages 99, 102)

5 dashes orange bitters

Add all ingredients to a shaker filled halfway with ice. Shake vigorously for about ten seconds. Strain the mixture into a glass filled with fresh ice. Garnish with a star anise.

Clavada de Chocolate

Throughout the pandemic, we welcomed patrons onto our patio even as the chill of winter set in, with temperatures dipping into the upper 20s and low 30s. Alongside propane heaters and handsome woolen blankets, we introduced a selection of warm cocktails. These became a favored choice during the colder months, offering our guests a delicious way to ward off the frosty air.

 1 oz. vodka

 4 oz. steamed oat milk

 1 oz. crème de cacao liqueur

 1 oz. almond liqueur

In the glass, combine all ingredients except for the oat milk; stir to mix. Steam and texture the oat milk, similar to preparing a cappuccino, and then pour it into the mixture. Garnish with three almonds on top.

Diplomáticos

The Diplomáticos cocktail takes its cue from bygone days of mid-20th-century diplomacy. It's a nod to when backroom banter and cozy corners of embassy lounges played as much a part in world affairs as the drinks poured to smooth the discussions.

1 ½ oz. white rum

1 oz. lime juice

½ oz. sweet vermouth

3 dashes bitters

½ oz. Campari

½ oz. organic blue agave

Add all ingredients to a shaker filled halfway with ice. Shake vigorously for about ten seconds. Strain the mixture into a glass. Garnish with a sprig of rosemary.

Dorado del Mar

This cocktail is a tribute to the enchanting beauty, inherent value, and captivating allure of the Caribbean Sea. It's a liquid ode to the serene yet profound essence of the deep waters that caress the shores of a myriad of islands, each with their unique tale.

1 ½ oz. dark rum

¾ oz. Campari

½ oz. demerara syrup
(page 97)

Add all ingredients to a shaker filled halfway with ice. Shake vigorously for about ten seconds. Strain the mixture into a glass filled with fresh ice. Garnish with a pineapple crown leaf.

Estreia

Estreia, a precursor to the iconic mojito, hails from the vibrant culture of Brazil. At its heart is cachaça, a spirit deeply ingrained in the social tapestry of Brazil and the star of its national cocktail, the Caipirinha. *Estreia*, meaning "debut" in Portuguese, celebrates the inaugural step toward the creation of many beloved cocktails, honoring the timeless tradition of cachaça.

2 oz. cachaça

5 mint leaves

¾ oz. lime juice

¾ oz. demerara syrup
(page 97)

Add all ingredients to a shaker filled halfway with ice. Shake vigorously for about ten seconds. Strain the mixture into a glass filled with fresh ice. Garnish with a lime wheel.

El Ultimo

El Ultimo holds a special place in our collection as the final summer cocktail creation served on the patio during the summer of 2022, when the Town of Vienna decided to close this cherished outdoor space. But there are no bitters in this drink. Instead, this cocktail was conceived as a tribute to the sun-drenched afternoons and the lively gatherings that once filled the air with laughter and conversation.

2 oz. tequila

¾ oz. demerara syrup (page 97)

1 oz. aguardiente

¾ oz. lime juice

Add all ingredients to a shaker filled halfway with ice. Shake vigorously for about ten seconds. Strain the mixture into a glass filled with fresh ice. Garnish with a lime wheel and a few mint leaves.

Gooseberry Smash

In many Latin American cultures, the gooseberry is not just a food item but a piece of heritage. It's often found when one meanders through local markets, with vendors proudly displaying the bright berries, a symbol of nature's simple luxuries. Our chef loved gooseberries, so we always had many.

2 oz. aguardiente

1 oz. organic blue agave

¾ oz. elderflower liqueur

1 oz. lemon juice

4 golden gooseberries

Add lemon juice and gooseberries to a shaker and use a muddler to gently press them down until their juices are released and they are lightly crushed. Next, fill the shaker with ice until it is halfway full. Place the remaining ingredients in the shaker. Shake vigorously for about ten seconds. Strain the mixture into a glass filled with fresh ice. For the garnish, take a single gooseberry with its husk intact and thread it onto a bamboo stick; place atop the drink.

Granada Brisa

The Granada Brisa is a tribute to Latin America's vibrant spirit, blending the rich, sweet depth of pomegranate with the bright citrus notes of Cointreau and fresh lime. This cocktail's heart is pure vodka, chosen for its clean taste that honors the boldness of the pomegranate. The addition of aquafaba introduces a creamy, frothy texture, a nod to the innovative culinary techniques that Latin America embraces, while ensuring the drink remains delightfully vegan.

3 oz. vodka

1 oz. lime juice

1 oz. Cointreau

1 oz. aquafaba (page 92)

1 oz. pomegranate purée (pages 99, 105)

Add all ingredients to a shaker filled halfway with ice. Shake vigorously for about ten seconds. Strain the mixture into a glass filled with fresh ice. Garnish with a sugarcane swizzle stick.

Jalisco Mule

When we first opened, we created many of our own infusions. This approach was excellent for experimenting with new flavors; however, it did not scale well given our volume and storage constraints. Luckily, we found many infused spirits that worked equally well in our cocktails. For simple recipes like this one, the quality of the mixer—ginger beer in this case—is also paramount.

2 oz. jalapeño-infused tequila

1 oz. sparkling water

½ oz. lime juice

3 oz. premium ginger beer

Place all ingredients into a copper mug filled with ice. Stir the mixture. Garnish with a half-length Hawaiian sugarcane swizzle stick.

Kiwi Caya

The spark for this cocktail ignited at a novel eatery in Aruba, where the zest of citrus harmonized with the island's balmy days and strong breezes. A whisper of agave melds into the blend, casting a sweet counterpoint to the citrus, orchestrating a refreshing rendition of the classic gin and tonic.

2 oz. gin

1 oz. lime juice

1 peeled kiwi

1 oz. premium tonic water

¾ oz. organic blue agave

In a cocktail shaker, muddle the kiwi with the gin and lime juice. Add the agave and fill the shaker halfway with ice. Shake vigorously for about ten seconds. Strain the mixture into a glass filled with fresh ice. Finish by adding tonic water. Garnish with a wedge of kiwi.

La Paloma

The classic cocktail recipe inspired our variant. We adhered closely to the original formulation, albeit with a change in the type of sweetener, while emphasizing the use of ultra-fresh citrus.

 2 oz. tequila

 6 mint leaves

 4 lime wedges

 ½ oz. organic blue agave

 2 grapefruit wedges

 ¾ oz. sparkling water

Apply salt to the outside of the glass*. In the glass, press together lime, grapefruit, and mint leaves to release their flavors. Fill the glass with ice, pour in the tequila and agave, and then complete with sparkling water. For garnish, add a pinch of salt and a sprig of mint.

* To salt the glass, moisten it with citrus and press into a plate of salt.

Los Roques

Los Roques, an archipelago off the coast of Venezuela, served as a muse for this cocktail, which captures its serene beauty and vibrant spirit. This cocktail is an homage to the tranquil yet lively essence of Los Roques, offering a taste of paradise in every sip, transporting one to the sun-kissed, sandy bliss of this South American jewel.

2 oz. dark rum

1 oz. lemon juice

1 oz. elderflower liqueur

½ oz. demerara syrup
(page 97)

Add all ingredients to a shaker filled halfway with ice. Shake vigorously for about ten seconds. Strain the mixture into a glass filled with fresh ice. Garnish with a sprig of mint.

Manzana Prohibida

Inspired under the crisp veil of fall patio evenings, this cocktail is a toast to simplicity. It's a breezy affair to assemble, yet each sip is a festive escapade. As autumn painted the town with its golden brush, we sought local Virginia apple cider.

2 ½ oz. bourbon

6 oz. apple cider

1 ½ oz. cinnamon syrup (page 94)

Gently warm the apple cider, carefully monitoring until it reaches about 130 degrees—just enough to release the cider's fragrant aroma without overheating. This method allows precise temperature control, ensuring the cider stays at a perfect sipping warmth. Once at temperature, blend in the cinnamon syrup and bourbon, stirring gently to marry the flavors. Serve with apple slices and a cinnamon stick garnish, inviting a swirl of spice with every sip.

Maravilla

We had a fondness for edible flowers, procuring them from local suppliers in Northern Virginia. For a while, we even cultivated our own mint and flowers from seeds in a small hydroponic farm. Flowers served as a fun garnish, adding a delightful touch to our cocktails (and many of our salads and desserts too).

 1 oz. tequila

 2 oz. pineapple purée (pages 99, 104)

 1 oz. mezcal

 ¼ oz. Grand Marnier

Add all ingredients to a shaker filled halfway with ice. Shake vigorously for about ten seconds. Strain the mixture into a glass. Garnish with an edible flower floating on the top of the cocktail.

Mario Bruijet Pisco Sour

Mario Alfonso Bruijet Burgos was a bartender at a Peruvian hotel in the 1920s and 1930s and is credited with popularizing the pisco sour. I altered his classic recipe by using aquafaba instead of egg whites to keep it plant-based and replacing white refined sugar with demerara.

2 oz. pisco

¾ oz. demerara syrup (page 97)

2 oz. aquafaba (page 92)

3 dashes bitters

1 oz. lime juice

Add all ingredients to a shaker filled halfway with ice. Shake vigorously for about ten seconds. Strain the mixture into a glass. Top with bitters.

Mojito Classico

The mojito is an emblematic of Cuban culture and tradition, celebrated in literature and music. It's a common feature in Cuban bars and cafés, and its refreshing nature makes it a popular choice in the hot Caribbean climate. I was fanatic about getting our mojito right, as there are a lot of poorly made mojitos in the world, bad copies of a cultural classic.

 2 oz. white rum

 10 fresh mint leaves

 2 oz. demerara syrup (page 97)

 1 oz. sparkling water

 1 large lime

Slice the lime thinly, removing and discarding the ends. Put the lime slices and mint in the shaker. Add the rum and demerara syrup. Muddle these ingredients together to release the lime's juices. Transfer the entire mixture into a glass filled with fresh ice. Fill the rest of the glass with sparkling water and stir thoroughly to mix. Garnish with a sugarcane stick and a sprig of mint.

Noche de Sueños

True to its name, which means "night of dreams," this cocktail is crafted for the evening unwind, promising the indulgence of a coffee cocktail without a hint of caffeine. In its creation, I turn to decaffeinated coffee beans processed with CO_2—a natural method that retains the deep flavors and aromatic allure of the coffee without the stimulant or chemical residue. The freshly roasted coffee also adds a lot to this drink.

1 ½ oz. dark rum

4 oz. oat milk

½ oz. coffee liqueur

2 oz. organic decaf espresso (page 96)

Prepare a latte mug by extracting 2 oz. of decaffeinated espresso. Add both dark rum and coffee liqueur and stir to combine. Steam the oat milk to 160 degrees while texturing. Gently pour the steamed oat milk into the mug over the espresso blend. Finish by topping the drink with a trio of espresso beans as garnish.

Nubes en el Viento

Some of our creative offerings were temporary highlights on the menu. One such example involved using cotton candy to create a cloud-like garnish that elegantly hovered over the drink. While this addition provided a novel taste experience, the process of making the cotton candy clouds was quite time-intensive. Due to the effort involved, we featured this unique touch on our menu for only a short time.

 1 ¼ oz. gin

 1 ¼ oz. sweet vermouth

 1 oz. Campari

 1 oz. Aperol

Add all ingredients to a shaker filled halfway with ice. Shake vigorously for about ten seconds. Strain the mixture into a glass filled with fresh ice. Garnish with a small tuft of cotton candy expertly shaped into a cloud and delicately placed on a bamboo stick in the drink.

Ocaso

Ocaso in Spanish translates to "sunset" or "twilight." It signifies that time of day when the sun sets and the light diminishes, the shift from day to night. Before we would get caught up in the evening's activities, we indulged in experimenting with new flavors at the bar. Therefore, it's the perfect name for this tropical cocktail that blends pomegranate, pineapple, coconut, and rum.

1 ½ oz. coconut rum

1 ½ oz. pomegranate purée
(pages 99, 105)

1 ½ oz. pineapple purée
(pages 99, 104)

Add all ingredients to a shaker filled halfway with ice. Shake vigorously for about ten seconds. Strain the mixture into a glass with fresh ice. Garnish with pineapple crown leaves.

Picoso

In this variation of a spicy margarita, a tequila base pays homage to sprawling agave fields, while chile liqueur infuses the drink with vibrant heat. A hint of Cointreau introduces a gentle citrus murmur, a subtle contrast to the lively spice. Demerara contributes a raw, unrefined sweetness, and the lime provides the zestful awakening that brings the entire sensory experience to life.

2 oz. tequila

½ oz. demerara syrup (page 97)

½ oz. chile liqueur

¾ oz. lime juice

½ oz. Cointreau

Add all ingredients to a shaker filled halfway with ice. Shake vigorously for about ten seconds. Strain the mixture into a glass with fresh ice. Garnish with green aji charapita peppers for a final flourish.

Picantarita

Though the recipe underwent two significant alterations, this cocktail remained on the menu from our opening day until the final service. This zesty tequila-based drink quickly became another favorite among our guests. Outside the summer watermelon season, we often used prickly pear purée. This produced a very similar flavor profile for the drink.

1 oz. jalapeño-infused tequila

½ oz. organic blue agave

¾ oz. chile liqueur

1 oz. lime juice

2 oz. juice from a fresh watermelon

Muddle the watermelon to extract the juice in shaker. Fill the shaker halfway with ice and add all other ingredients. Shake vigorously for about ten seconds. Strain the mixture into a glass filled with fresh ice. For garnish, place chile threads atop a lime wheel.

Quatro de Mora

Building on the success of our beloved gooseberry smash, I delved into crafting a new twist on that drink. This exploration led me to introduce four ripe blackberries into the mix, seeking a richer, deeper berry note. To complement this change, I selected an alternative sweetener that would harmonize with the blackberries' unique flavor.

2 oz. aguardiente

4 golden gooseberries

¾ oz. elderflower liqueur

4 blackberries

1 oz. lemon juice

1 oz. demerara syrup (page 97)

Add all ingredients to a shaker filled halfway with ice. Shake vigorously for about ten seconds. Strain the mixture into a glass over fresh ice. Garnish with a blackberry and mint leaves skewered on a bamboo stick to resemble a berry branch.

Sangria

When we first opened, everyone loved the bottled Spanish sangria we had on the menu. After we ran out, we made our own. We took a page out of the traditional Spanish recipe book and started mixing up a liter of sangria at a time. Sangria is an opportunity to mix different flavors to arrive at the perfect profile.

 4 oz. Spanish tempranillo red wine

 1 fresh orange

 2-3 fresh cherries

 1 oz. Cointreau

 ½ oz. organic blue agave

Rinse the orange and cherries, then slice the orange into wedges and pit and halve the cherries. In a mixing glass, stir together red wine, Cointreau, and agave until well mixed. Add the fruit and gently muddle. Pour into a glass with fresh ice, including the muddled fruit.

Side Note: If you want an easier alternative, you may use an organic fruit punch to replace the juice from the cherries and oranges. For a single glass, start with 2 oz. of juice and adjust to taste.

Smoke & Spice

This drink artfully blends rich apple cider with the smooth kick of tequila, while hints of lime and elderflower weave through the drink, creating a symphony of flavors. Each sip promises a gentle smokiness and a zesty spice that dances on the palate, offering a comforting embrace against crisp air.

1 ½ oz. reposado tequila

1 oz. apple cider

¾ oz. elderflower liqueur

½ oz. cinnamon syrup (page 94)

1 oz. lime juice

Add all ingredients to a shaker filled halfway with ice. Shake vigorously for about ten seconds. Strain the mixture into a glass. Garnish with two cinnamon sticks.

Spanish G&T

I find that the addition of citrus and adjusted proportions create a much more satisfying gin and tonic that reflects more of what I observed while traveling in Spain. The most enjoyable part of making this cocktail is layering the other flavors in the glass. I used juniper berries and rosemary, but you can create variants of this drink by adding various citrus peels and seasonally fresh ingredients and aromas.

2 oz. gin

5 oz. premium tonic water

½ fresh-squeezed lime

Place eight to twelve dried juniper berries into a glass. Crush ice and fill the glass until it is three-quarters full, creating a frosty bed for the liquids. Pour in the gin, followed by the fresh lime juice, and top it off with tonic water. Gently stir to meld the flavors together. Garnish with a sprig of rosemary, adding an aromatic dimension to the drink.

Tamarindo

Tamarind is a tropical fruit that originated in Africa but has been widely cultivated in Central and South America. The tamarind tree produces a pod-like fruit, which contains seeds encased in a sticky, tart pulp. The pulp is the edible part of the fruit and is highly prized for its sweet, sour, fruity flavor.

2 oz. bourbon

1 oz. aquafaba
(page 92)

2 oz. tamarind purée
(pages 99, 106)

½ oz. demerara syrup
(page 97)

Add all ingredients to a shaker filled halfway with ice. Shake vigorously for about ten seconds. Strain the mixture into a glass. Garnish by threading a Luxardo cherry onto a bamboo stick and placing it in the drink.

Trago de Limón

Sip on the essence of simplicity and sophistication with this refreshing cocktail that captures the spirit of effortless elegance. This crisp cocktail is a seamless blend of smooth vodka and the sweetly complex notes of Cointreau. A generous squeeze of fresh lemon adds a bright, citrusy zing balanced perfectly by the earthy sweetness of demerara sugar, lending a subtle molasses depth to the drink's profile.

2 oz. vodka

¾ oz. demerara syrup
(page 97)

¾ oz. Cointreau

1 oz. lemon juice

Add all ingredients to a shaker filled halfway with ice. Shake vigorously for about ten seconds. Strain the mixture into a glass. Garnish with a neat lemon twist, releasing a burst of citrus aroma to complement the cocktail's flavors. We often used Meyer lemons in the late fall and early winter.

Violeta

Chicha morada, a cherished beverage in Peru, is steeped in history and culture, crafted from an ancient variety of purple corn. We made chicha on-site with a traditional Peruvian recipe. Violeta marries the traditional beverage with the sophistication of modern mixology. The cocktail, with its purple hue, pays homage to Peru's vibrant and contemporary spirit.

1 oz. vodka

½ oz. elderflower liqueur

4 oz. chicha morada
(page 93)

Add all ingredients to a shaker filled halfway with ice. Shake vigorously for about ten seconds. Strain the mixture into a glass with ice. Garnish with a fresh lime wheel.

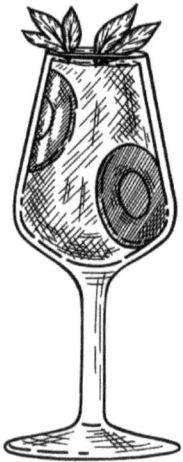

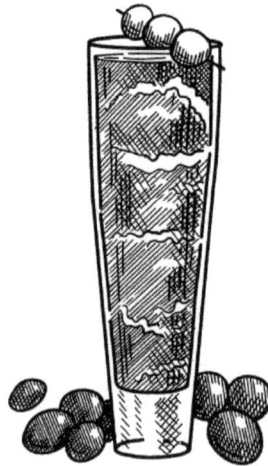

PART III

PREP

Aquafaba

Aquafaba, the liquid from canned chickpeas, has revolutionized the world of mixology by offering a plant-based substitute for egg whites in cocktails. This innovative ingredient has opened up new possibilities for vegan cocktails, allowing bartenders to recreate classic frothy drinks without compromising texture or taste. Its ability to whip up into a smooth, velvety foam has made it a popular choice for those seeking to indulge in the artistry of cocktails while adhering to vegan principles or managing egg allergies.

The discovery of aquafaba's unique properties has been a game-changer. Where egg whites are used to add body and create a silky mouthfeel in many shaken drinks, aquafaba performs admirably as a stand-in with its near-identical frothing capabilities. The transition from egg whites to aquafaba in cocktails is seamless, offering a consistency that is desirable in sours and fizz drinks. Its neutral taste ensures that the flavors of the spirits and mixers remain unaltered, preserving the cocktail's profile.

Embracing aquafaba not only accommodates dietary restrictions but also contributes to a more sustainable and waste-conscious approach. Traditionally, the brine from canned legumes might be poured down the sink without a second thought, but the repurposing of this liquid exemplifies a shift toward more eco-friendly practices.

Chicha Morada

Ingredients:

- 1 pound dried purple corn
- 1 gallon filtered water
- 1 stick cinnamon
- 1 cup white sugar
- 6 whole cloves
- 1 whole pineapple rind
- ½ cup fresh lime juice

Directions:

1. In a 10-quart pot, combine the corn, water, cinnamon stick, sugar, cloves, and pineapple rind.
2. Bring the mixture to a boil over high heat, then reduce the heat slightly but maintain a steady boil. Cook for approximately 30 minutes, stirring occasionally.
3. After cooking, allow the mixture to cool for 15 minutes. Then strain it using a chinois strainer to remove the solids.
4. Stir in ½ cup of lime juice.

Note:

The purple corn and pineapple rind can be reused. For subsequent batches, retain the corn and pineapple rind, adding fresh cinnamon, cloves, sugar, water, and lime juice. Repeat the boiling and straining process until the corn begins to break down. I always purchased the dried purple corn, in bags, from Latin markets. It is typically located in a packaged food isle.

Cinnamon Syrup

Ingredients:

- 1 cup white sugar
- 1 cup water
- 3 cinnamon sticks

Directions:

1. In a small saucepan, combine the sugar and water. Add the cinnamon sticks to the mixture.
2. Heat the saucepan over medium heat, stirring constantly until the sugar is fully dissolved.
3. Once the sugar is dissolved, reduce the heat to low and let the mixture simmer for about 10 minutes to infuse the cinnamon flavor.
4. Remove from the heat and allow the syrup to cool completely. Once cooled, remove the cinnamon sticks.

Note:

Transfer the cooled cinnamon syrup to a clean bottle or jar with a tight-fitting lid and store it in the refrigerator. The syrup should be used within 4 weeks for the best flavor.

Citrus

We always had a lot of fresh citrus at the bar, which is essential in crafting exceptional cocktails; its lively zest elevates each drink. We squeezed lemons and limes daily, capturing the fruit's vibrant oils and juices. Our storage containers often overflowed with grapefruits, oranges, and more exotic citrus varieties. For certain drinks, we'd press the citrus to order, ensuring peak freshness. The idea of using store-bought juice was out of the question.

The vibrant zing of fresh-squeezed lemon or lime juice is irreplaceable, offering a bright acidity that balances the sweetness of syrups and the warmth of spirits. Fresh citrus adds a complexity of flavor—a combination of tangy, bitter, and sweet—that bottled or concentrated juices simply cannot match. The aromatic oils in the zest, released when the fruit is cut or squeezed, also contribute a nuanced fragrance that enhances the drink's sensory appeal.

Beyond taste, the enzymatic properties of fresh lemon and lime juices play a subtle but significant role in the chemistry of cocktails. They can affect the texture and mouthfeel of a drink, sometimes adding a slight effervescence or acting as an emulsifier when shaken with other ingredients, like our aquafaba. This enzymatic activity begins to change and diminish over time, which is why using freshly squeezed juices is paramount for achieving the best taste and desired effect in a cocktail.

Bonus Recipe: We made our house lemonade with 2 oz. fresh-squeezed lemon juice, 2 oz. demerara syrup and 4 oz. of filtered, cold water—stir to combine well.

Coffee

Each week, I blended and roasted organic coffee on-site, ensuring that the coffee's flavor was fresh and robust. I carefully selected unroasted beans from a fair-trade importer that maintained partnerships with farmers in Central and South America. These partnerships focused on improving agricultural practices and crop quality to support both the product and the producers.

The freshness of the espresso beans was a critical factor in our coffee offering, and in the cocktails. It was standard practice to use beans that had been roasted that week. Aim for the ideal extraction time of approximately 25 seconds to produce a 2 oz. espresso shot from 20 grams of beans. This approach was fundamental in achieving a consistent and flavorful espresso with a proper crema on top.

Decaffeinated coffee options were also made available, matching the quality of regular beans to ensure that those who preferred or required less caffeine were given the same high-quality experience. The CO_2 decaf process, which utilizes compressed carbon dioxide to extract caffeine, preserves the distinct flavors and aromatic qualities of the coffee beans, resulting in a more flavor-rich decaffeinated coffee. This method also avoids the use of any chemical solvents and residuals in the beans.

Demerara Syrup

Ingredients:

- 1 cup demerara sugar
- 1 cup water

Directions:

1. In a medium saucepan, combine the demerara sugar with water.
2. Cook over medium heat and stir until the sugar has completely dissolved into the water. This should take about 3-5 minutes. Ensure that the mixture does not boil, as this can affect the syrup's consistency.
3. Once the sugar is dissolved, remove the saucepan from the heat and allow the syrup to cool to room temperature.

Essential Bar Tools

Boston shaker

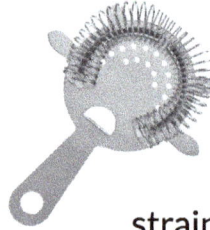
strainer

jigger

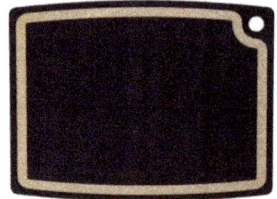
Epicurean cutting board

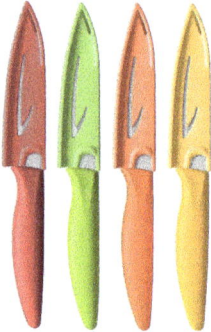
paring knives

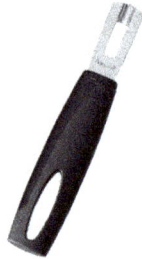
citrus peeler
and zester

bar spoon

muddler

ice mallet and bag

mixing glass

citrus press

Fruit Purées

Situated on the outskirts of Washington DC, we had a considerable challenge when it came to consistently sourcing tropical fruits that were up to par for our cocktails. In the beginning, my efforts to secure such quality ingredients led me on a journey through bustling markets imbued with Latin American flair and the aisles of local grocery stores peppered throughout the city. Occasionally I was fortunate enough to find the elusive perfect mango or an exemplary papaya. Yet, despite these sporadic victories, establishing a reliable standard for our cocktail quality proved to be arduous.

Tasting products from various commercial fruit purée providers, I discovered a wide selection of suppliers. However, upon closer inspection, many of these products included additional sugars and artificial flavors, which stood in stark contrast to the genuine taste profile I was committed to capturing.

That was until I discovered The Perfect Puree of Napa Valley. They offered frozen purées crafted from real fruit, with minimal added ingredients, truly embodying the diverse and natural flavors that I had long sought for our cocktail creations.

When the first batch of these purées arrived and I allowed them to thaw, the flavors were great. They were expensive, and I would have preferred fresh fruit; however, I found the cost justified by the unmatched flavor consistency.

Fruit Purées

I include the recipes for the purées, and based on where you are in the world, you may have more success finding quality fruit than I did.

Bonus Recipe: With these purées, I also made non-alcoholic *guarapos* that had 2 oz. fruit purée, 1 oz. organic blue agave, and 6 oz. sparkling water—stir to combine well.

Fruit Purée: Papaya

Ingredients:

- 1 medium ripe papaya
- 1 tablespoon fresh lime juice
- 1-2 teaspoons honey or sugar (optional, to taste)

Directions:

1. Begin by cutting the papaya in half lengthwise. Using a spoon, scoop out and discard the seeds.
2. Use a vegetable peeler or a knife to remove the skin from the papaya halves.
3. Chop the papaya flesh into small cubes and place them into a blender or food processor.
4. Add the fresh lime juice. The lime juice will not only add flavor but also help prevent the purée from oxidizing and turning brown.
5. Blend the mixture on high until smooth and homogeneous. If your papaya is particularly large or fibrous, you may need to pulse for a few minutes to achieve the right consistency.
6. Taste the purée and add honey or sugar a little at a time, blending and tasting after each addition until the desired sweetness is reached.
7. If the purée is too thick or the blender is having difficulty processing the papaya, add a tablespoon of water at a time until the desired consistency is achieved.
8. Pour the purée through a fine mesh sieve to remove any remaining fibers or chunks for a silky smooth texture.
9. Transfer the finished purée to an airtight container and refrigerate. Use within 3-4 days.

Fruit Purée: Passion Fruit

Ingredients:

- 10 ripe passion fruits
- ¼ cup cold water
(optional, depending on desired thickness)
- 2 tablespoons fine sugar (or to taste, optional)
- A pinch of salt

Instructions:

1. Begin by cutting the passion fruits in half.
2. Over a medium-sized bowl, scoop out the passion fruit pulp and seeds with a spoon. Be sure to scrape the inside of the rind to get all the pulp.
3. (Optional) For a smoother purée, strain the pulp through a fine mesh sieve into another bowl. Use the back of a spoon to push through as much pulp as possible.
5. Add the passion fruit pulp back into the bowl. Stir in the cold water to reach your desired consistency—the purée should be thick yet pourable.
6. Sweeten with fine sugar, adding a tablespoon at a time, tasting as you go. Keep in mind that the sweetness of the passion fruit can vary, so you may need more or less sugar.
7. Add a pinch of salt to enhance the flavors. Stir well until the salt and sugar completely dissolve.
8. Transfer the purée to an airtight container. It will keep in the refrigerator for up to a week.

Fruit Purée: Pink Guava

Ingredients:

- 1 medium ripe pink guava
- 1 tablespoon fresh lime juice
- 1-2 teaspoons honey or sugar (optional, to taste)

Directions:

1. Begin by cutting the pink guava in half lengthwise. Using a spoon, scoop out and discard the black seeds from the center.
2. Use a vegetable peeler or a knife to remove the skin from the pink guava halves.
3. Chop the pink guava flesh into small cubes and place them into a blender or food processor.
4. Add the fresh lime juice to the pink guava in the blender. The lime juice will not only add flavor but also help prevent the purée from oxidizing and turning brown.
5. Blend the mixture on high until it becomes smooth and homogeneous. If your pink guava is particularly large or fibrous, you may need to pulse for a few minutes to achieve the right consistency.
6. Taste the purée and decide if you need to add any sweetener. If the pink guava is not as sweet as you'd like, add honey or sugar a little at a time, blending and tasting after each addition until the desired sweetness is reached.
7. If the purée is too thick or the blender is having difficulty processing the pink guava, you can add a tablespoon of water at a time until the desired consistency is achieved.
8. Pour the purée through a fine mesh sieve to remove any remaining fibers or chunks for a silky smooth texture.
9. Transfer the finished purée to an airtight container and refrigerate. Use within 3-4 days.

Fruit Purée: Pineapple

Ingredients:

- 1 large ripe pineapple
- 2 teaspoons freshly squeezed lime juice
- 1-2 tablespoons sugar (optional, depending on the sweetness of the pineapple)
- ¼ cup water (if needed for blending)

Directions:

1. Peel the pineapple, removing all the eyes and the core. Chop the fruit into chunks small enough to blend smoothly.
2. Place the pineapple chunks into a blender. Add the fresh lime juice, which will not only add flavor but also help prevent oxidation and browning.
3. Blend the mixture at high speed until smooth. If your pineapple is a bit fibrous, you might need to blend for a minute or two for a completely smooth consistency.
4. Taste the purée. Depending on the sweetness of the pineapple, you may want to add sugar to taste. If you add sugar, blend again to ensure it's fully dissolved.
5. If the purée is too thick or if your blender struggles to process the pineapple, add water, a tablespoon at a time, until the desired consistency is reached.
6. Strain the purée through a fine mesh sieve to remove any remaining fibrous bits, using the back of a spoon to press all the liquid through.
7. Transfer the purée to an airtight container and refrigerate. Use within 4-5 days.

Fruit Purée: Pomegranate

Ingredients:

- 2 large pomegranates
- ¼ cup water or pomegranate juice (optional, for adjusting consistency)
- 1-2 tablespoons sugar (optional, to taste)
- 1 teaspoon lemon juice
(to stabilize color and add a zesty note)

Directions:

1. Slice the pomegranates in half horizontally. Hold each half over a deep bowl, cut-side down, and tap the skin firmly with a wooden spoon. The seeds should fall out into the bowl. Remove any pith that falls in as well.
2. Transfer the seeds to a blender.
3. Pulse the seeds until they break down and release their juice. Avoid over-blending to prevent breaking down the bitter inner seed.
4. Pour the blended mixture through a fine mesh sieve or cheesecloth over a bowl. Use the back of a spoon or a spatula to press the pulp and extract as much juice as possible.
5. To the strained liquid, add the lemon juice, and if you desire a sweeter taste, add sugar incrementally, tasting as you go until the desired sweetness is achieved.
6. If the purée is too thick, adjust the consistency by adding a little water or pomegranate juice.
7. Transfer it to an airtight container and refrigerate. It should keep well for up to a week.

Fruit Purée: Tamarind

Ingredients:

- 1 cup tamarind pods
- 2 cups hot water
- ¼ cup sugar (optional to taste)
- A pinch of salt

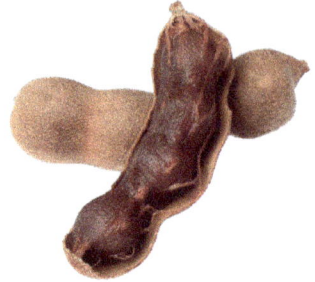

Directions:

1. Start by peeling the tamarind pods. Remove the outer husk and discard any strings attached to the pulp.
2. Place the tamarind pulp into a large bowl. Pour the hot water over the pulp, ensuring that it is fully submerged. Let it soak for about 1 hour, or until the pulp softens and breaks down easily.
3. After soaking, use your hands or a spoon to mash the pulp in the water to separate the flesh from the seeds.
4. Once the pulp is thoroughly mashed, strain the mixture through a fine mesh sieve into another bowl. Press the pulp against the sieve to extract as much liquid as possible. The seeds and fibrous parts should be left behind.
5. To the strained tamarind liquid, add sugar and salt. Stir well until sugar is fully dissolved. Adjust the sweetness to your taste; tamarind has a natural sourness that can be balanced with the sugar.
6. If the purée is too thick, add a little water to reach the desired consistency.
7. Transfer to an airtight container and store it in the refrigerator. Use within a week.

Garnish

The garnish on a cocktail plays a significant role beyond mere decoration, contributing to both the aesthetic and the taste of the beverage. It is a deliberate finishing detail that can subtly influence the flavor profile and aroma as well as provide a visual cue to the nature of the drink. Skillfully chosen, a garnish aligns with the drink's character, ensuring that each element is in harmony, and this attention to detail marks a well-crafted cocktail. A small food dehydrator is also a worthy investment to make dehydrated citrus and other fruit which can also be charred for a completely different look to a drink.

Here is a garnish checklist covering every cocktail in this book; it's also a list of interesting items to have at your bar.

-Almonds
-Apple slices
-Bee pollen
-Blackberries
-Candied ginger
-Chile dust
-Chile threads
-Cinnamon sticks
-Cotton candy
-Dehydrated blood orange wheel
-Dried juniper berries
-Edible flowers
-Espresso beans
-Fresh mint
-Gooseberry with husk
-Green aji charapita peppers
-Kiwi slice
-Lemon wheel

-Lime wheel
-Maraschino cherries
-Meyer lemon twist
-Pineapple crown leaves
-Rosemary sprig
-Star anise
-Sugarcane swizzle stick

Ice

In cocktails, ice is far more than just a cooling element; it's essential for balancing flavor and enhancing the overall taste. Different ice shapes, like large spheres or cubes, melt slowly, reducing dilution and adding sophistication, whereas crushed ice quickly chills and dilutes, blending intense flavors smoothly. While I had a machine for small cubed ice, we sourced large ice from suppliers and grocery stores. Making clear large ice was inconsistent without commercial equipment. For crushed ice, we used a canvas bag and crushed it with a mallet.

Milk (Oat)

As an early adopter of oat milk as a dairy alternative, I valued its long shelf life and its fitness for dairy-free diets. However, I quickly learned the importance of examining oat milk varieties more closely. Many contain added oils to emulate the creamy texture of dairy milk. This discovery led to a more careful selection process, seeking oat milk that offered a balance between desirable texture and natural, wholesome ingredients. There are also "barista" versions of oat milk that are optimized for texturing and frothing, and while these work well, many have undesirable oils.

Water (Sparkling)

One of the most lavish investments that few guests cared about was our water. Up until our final months, we had one of the most cutting-edge water filtration systems on the planet. This state-of-the-art system didn't just guarantee impeccably clean water; it also dispensed effervescent sparkling water for all our cocktails, avoiding the need to purchase bottled water. It served as an essential component in our beverage creation process, meticulously eliminating a comprehensive array of impurities ranging from minuscule microplastics to other subtle contaminants. The system ensured that our water, which served as an ingredient in many of our cocktails, was of unparalleled purity.

Wine

For our cocktails, we adopted a sustainable approach to utilize leftover wine from the previous evening's service. A quality base wine is fundamental to the flavor and integrity of certain cocktails, leading us to repurpose this leftover wine as a key ingredient in our mixology. This practice not only was environmentally responsible but also ensured that our cocktails had a unique and refined taste profile. We were particularly careful in our selection of wines, using only 100% organic options to align with our commitment to quality and sustainability.

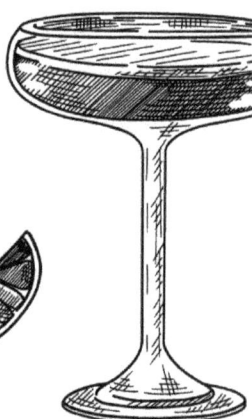
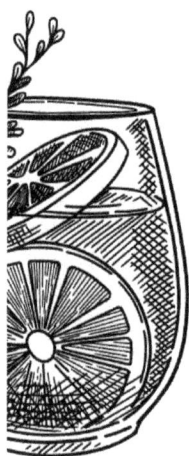

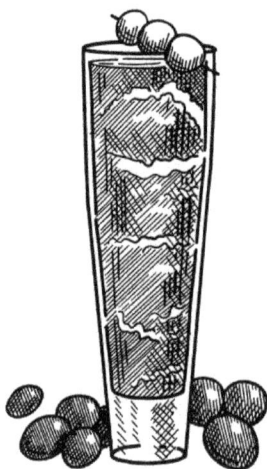

PART IV

SPIRITS

Aguardiente

In the rich and varied world of distilled spirits, aguardiente holds a special place, especially in its Colombian form. This term, a blend of the Spanish words for "water," *agua*, and "fire," *ardiente*, generally refers to a type of distilled spirit. The Colombian variant of aguardiente sets itself apart with its notable simplicity and the unique addition of anise, characteristics that make it exceptionally well suited for crafting innovative cocktails. Distinct from many other spirits, aguardiente is characterized by its lack of aging, which preserves a pure and clear taste profile, thereby enhancing its versatility for blending with other ingredients in a variety of drinks.

In the context of Colombian culture, aguardiente transcends being merely a beverage; it is woven into the societal fabric, particularly in the Andean region. It embodies more than the sum of its parts—it is a potent symbol of national identity and cultural pride. Aguardiente's capacity to evolve while maintaining its essential qualities reflects the dynamic and fluid nature of Latin American societies. This spirit is not just a relic of the past; it is an active part of Latin America's present and future, continually influencing and being influenced by the region's rich and ever-changing cultural landscape.

Almond Liqueur

As a widely recognized and appreciated liqueur, amaretto holds a special place in the hearts of many connoisseurs. Among the various brands available, one name that particularly stands out is Disaronno. This delightful spirit is known for its sweet, rich flavor, which is often attributed to almonds. However, the secret behind its unique taste often lies in the use of apricot pits, which provide a distinctive almond-like aroma and flavor. The use of apricot in Disaronno contributes to its smoothness and depth of flavor. This ingredient choice reflects a commitment to maintaining the authenticity of the traditional amaretto while offering a distinct character.

Side Note: A liqueur is a type of alcoholic beverage that is typically sweet and flavored with a variety of ingredients, such as fruits, herbs, spices, flowers, nuts, or cream. Unlike distilled spirits like whiskey or vodka, liqueurs are usually not aged for a long period, though they may rest for a short time to allow their flavors to meld. The key characteristics of liqueurs include:

1. **Flavoring**: Liqueurs are distinguished by their unique and often complex flavors. These flavors are derived from the specific ingredients used in their production. Common examples include fruit-based liqueurs like limoncello or cherry liqueur, herb-based ones like Jägermeister or Chartreuse, and cream-based options like Bailey's Irish Cream.
2. **Sweetening**: Liqueurs are generally quite sweet. They are often sweetened with sugar, syrup, or other sweeteners, which not only contributes to the flavor but also helps to balance the intensity of other ingredients.
3. **Alcohol Content**: The alcohol content in liqueurs can vary widely but is typically lower than that of pure distilled spirits.

Amaro Averna

For over a century and a half, a unique bitter Sicilian aperitif has been captivating palates with its rich and complex flavors. The foundation of this delightful beverage lies in the sun-kissed bitter oranges that thrive in the Sicilian landscape. These oranges, known for their distinctively sharp yet aromatic profile, provide the aperitif with its characteristic citrusy base, a true testament to the region's bountiful orchards.

But the secret to this aperitif's allure doesn't end with citrus. A handpicked assortment of herbs and roots, each with its own unique properties and flavors, is meticulously blended into the mix. These botanicals infuse the aperitif with layers of depth, creating an intricate tapestry of tastes that dance on the palate. This harmonious blend of herbs and roots has been perfected over the years, ensuring that each sip offers a journey through the essence of Sicily's natural splendor.

Ancho Reyes Chile Liqueur (Red)

Ancho Reyes is a distinctive chile liqueur from Puebla City, Mexico, and is produced based on a recipe dating back to 1927. It is crafted from Puebla's renowned ancho chiles, which are the dried form of ripe poblano peppers. The red chiles are sun-dried for 15 to 20 days, transforming their vegetal notes into rich, baking-spice-like notes. These chiles are then left to soak in small vats of neutral cane spirit from Veracruz, Mexico, for half a year. Following this, the infused liquid is hand-blended by a master blender to ensure consistent flavor and spice.

Angostura Bitters

Angostura bitters, a name synonymous with classic cocktail crafting, has a rich history that dates back to the early 19th century. In 1824, Dr. Johann Siegert, a German surgeon general in the army of Simón Bolívar, first created what was then known as *amargo aromático* in Angostura, Venezuela. Originally developed as a medicinal tincture to alleviate stomach ailments, it gradually gained popularity as a cocktail enhancer. Though it is typically used as an accent, some bartenders are increasing the amount of Angostura to use it as a base spirit. I also use Angostura's orange bitters, a variant made from the peels of sun-ripened Caribbean oranges grown in Trinidad. These oranges are handpicked by select growers and harvested only during the rainy season to ensure optimal freshness and flavor.

Aperol

Since the dawn of the 20th century, the production of Aperol, a renowned Italian aperitif, has been a meticulous art. The process begins with the infusion of a carefully curated collection of botanicals into a high-quality alcohol base. This base, often vodka or a neutral grain spirit, serves as a pristine canvas, eagerly awaiting the rich, vibrant hues of flavor from the botanicals.

The heart of Aperol's distinctiveness lies in the infusion process, initiated through the careful maceration of various botanicals. This diverse mix includes sweet and bitter oranges, an array of herbs, and roots such as rhubarb and gentian. The maceration process is a delicate dance of time and flavor, allowing the botanicals to impart their essence into the alcohol. This gradual infusion is key to achieving the harmonious blend that forms the soul of Aperol's flavor.

Following the infusion, the now flavor-rich alcohol undergoes further blending with additional alcohol and water. The mixture is then filtered to eliminate any impurities, ensuring clarity and purity in every bottle. At this juncture, sugar and other flavorings are introduced, artfully balancing the sweetness with the inherent bitterness derived from the botanicals. This careful calibration results in Aperol's signature taste, which is notably sweeter and less alcoholic than that of its counterpart, Campari.

Bourbon

Whisky and bourbon, while related, have distinct production processes and regulations that set them apart. Bourbon, a type of whiskey, must be produced in the United States and adhere to specific legal requirements. The grain mixture for bourbon must contain at least 51% corn, which imparts a sweeter profile compared to the broader range of grains used in other whiskies. Bourbon's fermentation process involves converting sugars to alcohol, creating a "wash." This is then distilled and aged in new, charred oak barrels, a requirement unique to bourbon. These barrels impart deep flavors of caramel and vanilla, distinguishing bourbon's flavor profile from those of other whiskies, which may be aged in uncharred or previously used barrels, leading to a wider variety of flavors and complexities.

I normally selected Bulleit, a brand well recognized in the world of spirits. Although there are many outstanding bourbon producers, Bulleit has carved out its own niche. The brand traces its roots back to the 1830s, when the original creator, Augustus Bulleit, crafted the first batch. His great-great-grandson, Tom Bulleit, revived the brand in 1987, adhering closely to Augustus's original high-rye recipe. This recipe, consisting of 68% corn, 28% rye, and 4% malted barley, is known for its bold and spicy character. The bourbon's unique flavor profile is further enhanced by special strains of yeast and pure Kentucky limestone-filtered water, contributing to its subtlety and complexity.

Cachaça

In the lush agricultural heartlands of Brazil, the craft of cachaça production is a cherished tradition dating back to the 1600s. The journey of this distinctive spirit begins with the manual harvesting of sugarcane, a process steeped in history. These freshly cut canes are quickly taken to mills, where they are processed to extract the sweet sugarcane juice, that forms the essence of artisanal cachaça.

This sugarcane juice then embarks on a brief journey in fermentation vats, where yeast is added. Over the next 24 to 48 hours, the yeast works its magic, converting the sugars into alcohol, resulting in a low-alcohol wine. This step is crucial in defining the primary character of cachaça. Following fermentation, the wine undergoes distillation in copper stills, a choice material for its sulfur-removing qualities. This process not only intensifies the alcohol content but also purifies the liquid, with only the heart cut—the portion with ideal flavors and alcohol strength—being reserved for cachaça.

The final chapter in cachaça's creation is its categorization into unaged (white) or aged (gold) variants. The unaged cachaça is typically bottled and sold immediately post-distillation, capturing the spirit in its most primal form.

Meanwhile, the aged cachaça embarks on a maturation journey in wooden barrels, acquiring a complex flavor profile and a golden hue over time. The choice of wood for the barrels and the aging duration profoundly influence the final taste and appearance of the cachaça, marking each batch with its unique signature.

Campari

Campari, an iconic Italian aperitif, has intrigued palates since the mid-1800s with its striking red hue and unique blend of flavors. Crafted from a secret recipe dating back to 1860, its composition is known only to a few. The liqueur's rich flavor profile is derived from an infusion of herbs and spices, including bitter orange, rhubarb, ginseng, and cascarilla bark, combined with alcohol and water. This blend of ingredients gives Campari its distinctive character.

The production process of Campari starts with steeping dry botanicals in water, followed by mixing them with alcohol and more water. This mixture is then left to macerate over an extended period, allowing for the full extraction of flavors. The resulting base is a brown liquid that undergoes further refinement, including the addition of sugar and a coloring agent, to achieve its signature bright red color and balanced taste profile. The final product's alcohol content varies depending on the market it is intended for, with a typical range of 20.5% to 28.5% ABV.

Side Note: A curaçao is a broad category of orange liqueurs. Campari, Aperol, Grand Marnier, and Cointreau are all types of curaçaos, and each played a large and distinctive role in our cocktails. While in a pinch you could swap one for another, they have distinctive flavor characteristics that add many unique traits to the drinks.

Chartreuse (Yellow)

The production of Yellow Chartreuse, a well-regarded French liqueur, unfolds through a process blending ancient monastic traditions with modern distillation techniques. The journey begins with a careful selection of botanicals. At least 130 different plants and flowers are chosen to create the unique and complex flavor profile of Yellow Chartreuse. These botanicals are macerated in a high-quality neutral spirit, initiating the extraction of their essences, a crucial step that lays the foundation for the liqueur's distinctive taste and aroma.

Following maceration, the botanical-infused spirit is subjected to a distillation process. The spirit and botanical mixture is distilled in traditional copper alembic stills, a practice steeped in the heritage of French spirit production. This distillation not only purifies the spirit but also concentrates the flavors, ensuring that the essence of the botanicals is finely captured within the liquid. The resultant distillate, now imbued with the characteristics of the selected botanicals, is a step closer to becoming the revered Yellow Chartreuse.

The final act in the production of Yellow Chartreuse is the aging process. The liqueur is aged in oak barrels, allowing it to develop and mature over time. The interaction between the liquid and the wood enriches the liqueur, imparting it with additional flavors and a smooth texture. During this aging period, the liqueur also acquires its signature yellow color, distinguishing it from its green counterpart.

Cherry Liqueur (Luxardo)

Luxardo's exceptional liqueurs owe their distinctive taste to the marasca cherries cultivated around the Luxardo estate in Italy. The meticulous use of every part of the cherry—fruit, pits, leaves, and stems—contributes to an unparalleled depth of flavor. The initial preparation stage involves carefully cleaning and mashing the cherries and combining them with select botanicals, setting the groundwork for a rich extraction of flavors and essential compounds that define the liqueur's spirit.

The next phase involves soaking the cherry mixture in a neutral spirit. This step is crucial, as it allows for the full extraction of the essential flavors and compounds from the cherries and botanicals. Following this infusion process, the mixture undergoes distillation in traditional stills. This distillation process is carefully monitored to ensure the purity and intensity of the flavors, capturing the essence of the Luxardo cherries while removing any impurities.

The final stage is the maturation in ashwood vats. The duration of this aging process is adjusted according to the desired flavor profile and characteristics of each batch of liqueur. This aging not only enhances the depth and complexity of the flavors but also allows for a harmonious blend of the various components. Once the liqueur has matured to perfection, it undergoes a final filtration process. This step is followed by necessary adjustments, such as sweetening or coloring, to meet the exact specifications of the final product.

Coffee Liqueur

The creation of coffee liqueur starts with selecting superior coffee beans, typically from high-altitude regions famous for their robust flavors. These beans undergo precise roasting to enhance their full flavor potential. Once roasted, they're ground and steeped in water, creating a rich coffee base essential for the liqueur's foundation.

This intense coffee extract is then carefully mixed with a spirit, such as vodka or rum, to add depth and complexity. The type of spirit chosen subtly influences the liqueur's final taste. To counter the coffee's bitterness, sweeteners like sugar or syrup are added. The precise ratios of coffee, alcohol, and sweetener are proprietary secrets, contributing to each brand's distinct flavor profile.

The blend then enters a maturation stage, when the flavors meld and mellow. The duration of aging varies, with some brands opting for a brief period to maintain the coffee's boldness, while others age longer for enhanced complexity. After aging, the liqueur is filtered, ensuring a clear, smooth final product that encapsulates the essence of rich, aromatic coffee.

Cointreau

The meticulously sourced orange peels are the cornerstone of Cointreau's unique and recognizable taste. These peels, derived from a curated blend of sweet and bitter oranges, undergo a rigorous selection process. The sweet orange peels contribute a burst of fresh, sugary zest, offering a light and vibrant note. In contrast, the bitter orange peels lend a sophisticated and multi-dimensional depth to the liqueur. This harmonious combination creates a rich and complex citrus profile that is both unique and integral to Cointreau's identity.

Each peel is removed manually, ensuring that only the most fragrant and flavorful parts of the orange are utilized. This manual peeling process is labor-intensive and meticulous, reflecting the brand's respect for artisanal methods that have been passed down through generations. Once peeled, the orange skins are then sun-dried, a method that naturally intensifies their essential oils. This drying process enhances the liqueur with robust, concentrated citrus flavors, giving Cointreau its distinctive and vibrant character. This blend of carefully chosen ingredients and traditional production techniques not only infuses Cointreau with its celebrated flavor but also bridges the contemporary product with a legacy of artisanal craftsmanship.

Crème de Cacao (Tempus Fugit)

The journey of this liqueur starts in the verdant rainforests of Venezuela, where cacao beans are sourced for their rich and nuanced flavor profile. The vanilla, sourced from the fragrant expanses of Mexico, adds its own historical charm. Mexican vanilla has been a sought-after spice since the 19th century, renowned for its unique aroma and flavor.

The crafting of Tempus Fugit Crème de Cacao begins with the meticulous distillation of these raw cacao beans. This process, marrying both art and scientific precision, aims to capture the purest essence of the cacao, ensuring that every drop of the liqueur resonates with the bean's original depth and complexity.

The freshly distilled cacao spirit is then infused with an additional batch of cacao and whole vanilla beans. The beans are carefully crushed, a process that releases their aromatic oils and essence, creating a rich tapestry of scents and tastes. This step is crucial in achieving the liqueur's intricate flavor profile, where the robust, earthy notes of cacao blend seamlessly with the sweet, alluring undertones of vanilla. As this fusion occurs, the liqueur gradually adopts its distinctive medium brown hue, an aesthetic nod to the chocolates and desserts that it is meant to evoke.

Elderflower Liqueur

Elderflower liqueur is a spirit embodying the subtle yet enchanting aroma of elderflower blossoms. These blooms, handpicked during the height of their fragrant late spring bloom, are essential for capturing the unique, sweetly floral essence. This meticulous harvesting reflects a deep commitment to quality, with the timing of the pick being a critical factor in preserving the peak flavors of the flowers.

The heart of the liqueur's production lies in its infusion process. Fresh elderflower blossoms are submerged in a neutral spirit, initiating a period of steeping whose duration is a closely guarded secret of each producer. This stage is pivotal, as it determines the depth and intensity of the flavor extracted from the flowers. After the flowers are removed, the infusion is sweetened with sugar to create a luxuriously rich syrup. This syrup, carefully balanced for sweetness and alcohol content, captures the delicate floral notes that define the liqueur's signature profile.

Completing the elderflower liqueur requires a meticulous blending process. The sweetened elderflower infusion is combined with additional spirits and sometimes water to achieve the desired alcohol strength. Often, the liqueur is allowed to age for a short time, a step that lets the flavors marry and mellow. This aging process ensures a smoother, more refined taste.

Gin

Gin production begins with the juniper berry, defining its signature flavor. A careful selection of botanicals such as coriander seeds, citrus peels, angelica root, and orris root is made, each contributing to the gin's unique flavor and aromatic profile.

In the distillation phase, the blend of grain spirit and botanicals is heated in copper alembic stills. This heating causes the essential oils and flavors from the botanicals to evaporate, ascending through the still to the cooling condenser. Here, they transform back into liquid, now imbued with the complex botanical essences. This distillation is often repeated multiple times, refining the spirit and intensifying its flavor and purity.

Post-distillation, the gin undergoes a rigorous quality assessment to ensure consistency and excellence. Some gins may enter an aging process to further develop their flavors, but many are bottled right after distillation.

I chose Hendrick's gin for the bar, a distinctively crafted spirit known for its unique and somewhat unconventional flavor profile. Launched in 1999 by William Grant & Sons in Girvan, Scotland, Hendrick's is made using a blend of traditional gin botanicals like juniper, coriander, and citrus peel, but it's distinguished by its signature infusions of cucumber and Bulgarian rose. This combination yields a refreshingly floral and slightly sweet flavor, setting it apart from more traditional gins.

Grand Marnier

Grand Marnier's crucial component is fine cognac produced from grapes grown in France's Charente region. This cognac is expertly blended with distilled orange liqueur, forming the core of the flavor profile. Sugar syrup is added, providing the liqueur a smoother, more palatable finish. This meticulous combination results in a unique 40% ABV liqueur celebrated for its seamless blend of citrus and cognac distinctively free from added herbs or spices.

The first distillery was established in 1827 by Jean Baptiste Lapostolle in Neauphle-le-Château. Years later, in 1876, his granddaughter Julia married Louis-Alexandre Marnier, marking a pivotal moment in the brand's history. It was in 1880 that Alexandre Marnier-Lapostolle, inspired by the then-popular orange liqueurs, created his own version using cognac as the base and adding wild oranges from Haiti, giving birth to what was initially called Curaçao Marnier. This blend quickly gained popularity among locals and tourists alike. In 1887, the Grand Marnier Cordon Rouge was introduced and became a symbol of French luxury and sophistication, remaining largely unchanged to this day.

Mezcal

Mezcal, a traditional Mexican spirit, is categorized into three distinct types, each with its own unique production methods and characteristics. The first category is simply known as mezcal, which is made from 100% agave. In this category, producers are allowed to add water, cultured yeasts, and other products during the fermentation process. This flexibility in ingredients and production methods results in a wide range of flavors and styles within this category, and this is typically a good base for cocktails.

The second category, Mezcal *artesanal*, emphasizes a more traditional approach to production. In this category, the agave is typically roasted in underground pits, giving the mezcal its distinctive smoky flavor. Water may be added during the production process, but the focus remains on maintaining traditional methods and flavors.

Mezcal *ancestral* represents the most traditional and rigorous category of mezcal production. In this category, the agave must be cooked in underground pits, and the roasted agave hearts are required to be shredded by hand, followed by natural fermentation. This adherence to ancient production techniques ensures a high level of authenticity and quality.

Beyond these three primary categories, additional classifications exist based on aging and whether flavoring or other ingredients have been added. These classifications allow for a diverse range of mezcals, each with its own unique identity and flavor profile.

Pisco

Pisco is a type of brandy produced in Peru and Chile. The spirit is distilled from a variety of grapes, which are grown specifically for pisco production. In Peru, the production is often from a single grape variety, resulting in what is known as a *puro*, or from a blend, creating an *acholado*. In Chile, it is more common to see piscos made from the Muscat grape. The selected grapes are crucial in defining the spirit's ultimate profile, with each varietal imparting its unique flavors and aromas.

The production process begins with the harvesting of the grapes, which are pressed to extract their juice. The juice is then allowed to ferment, converting the natural sugars into alcohol, a process that can last from one to two weeks. This results in a grape must or *mosto*, which is then ready for distillation. Pisco is traditionally distilled in copper pot stills, which allows for precise control over the distillation process. In Peru, the distillation is done only once, with the entire output captured without making cuts for heads or tails, which contributes to pisco's distinct flavor profile.

After distillation, Peruvian pisco must rest for a minimum of three months in vessels that do not alter its properties, such as stainless steel or glass, a regulation that ensures the pure expression of the grape's flavors. Chilean pisco can be aged in wood, which may impart additional characteristics to the spirit. Neither variant of pisco is allowed to have any additives, ensuring that the final product is a clear, pure expression of the distilled grape juice.

Rum

Rum's creation begins with sugarcane, the plant at its heart. It's either the fresh juice of sugarcane or molasses, a by-product of sugar refining, that serves as the base for fermentation. This ingenious use of sugarcane derivatives for alcohol production dates back to the 17th-century Caribbean, marking the genesis of rum as it is known today.

During the distillation phase. the fermented base is refined to enhance its alcohol content and develop its distinct flavor profile. However, it's the aging process that truly defines rum's character. Stored in wooden barrels, the rum undergoes a transformation, absorbing elements from the wood. This interaction during aging contributes to the rum's color, flavor, and complexity.

The length of aging can vary significantly, from a few years to several decades, with longer periods typically yielding deeper, more intricate flavors. The type of wood used for the barrels also plays a crucial role. For instance, oak barrels often impart a smooth vanilla note to the rum, while other woods can introduce more exotic flavors. Over time, the rum develops a balanced and harmonious profile, a reflection of both the environment in which it's aged and the artistry of its makers.

Singani

Singani is a distinctive spirit that hails from the high valleys of Bolivia, and it represents a category of distilled alcohol that is specific to the region. It is made from the aromatic white Muscat of Alexandria grape, which, when grown at the high altitudes characteristic of Bolivian vineyards, develops a unique flavor profile.

The production process begins with the careful cultivation of the grapes at altitudes above 5,250 feet, where the diurnal temperature variation is significant and the soil is minerally rich. Once harvested, the grapes are crushed to create a must, which is then fermented using natural yeasts. This fermentation process is meticulously monitored to preserve the natural flavors and aromas inherent in the Muscat grapes. The fermented must is then distilled, typically using copper stills that contribute to the spirit's smoothness and complexity. The production of singani uses traditional distillation methods, which involves a single distillation process to capture the purest expression of the grape's character.

After distillation, singani undergoes a resting period before bottling to allow its flavors to meld. Unlike many other spirits, singani does not require aging in wooden barrels, which ensures that the final product maintains the clear, clean taste that reflects the grape's qualities and the distinctive minerality of the Bolivian terroir.

Tequila

Tequila, a well-known Mexican spirit, is a specific regional variant of mezcal. It is closely associated with the region of Jalisco, Mexico, a geographical indication that is integral to its identity and production. This regional specificity distinguishes tequila from other forms of mezcal produced in different parts of Mexico. At its core, tequila maintains blue agave as its primary ingredient, a characteristic that defines its unique flavor profile and distinguishes it from other spirits.

The production process of tequila involves a double distillation of the blue agave. This meticulous process is crucial for refining the spirit and achieving the desired purity and taste. Tequila's composition can vary: while it can be made entirely from agave, there are also versions that incorporate sugars from other sources, such as sugarcane. This variation in ingredients contributes to the diversity of flavors and styles found within the category of tequila.

Among the various types of tequila, *reposados* and *añejos* are notable for their aging process. Reposado tequilas are aged in oak barrels for up to two years, a process that imparts a smoothness and complexity to the spirit. In contrast, añejo tequilas undergo a longer aging period, extending over two years. This extended aging process results in a tequila with even greater depth of flavor, complexity, and richness, distinguishing añejos as a premium category within the world of tequila.

Vermouth (Sweet)

Sweet vermouth, an integral member of the fortified and aromatized wine category, is enriched by an array of herbs, spices, and botanical elements. My preference leans toward a brand from Marseillan, France, a choice influenced by a memorable visit to their production center. This visit offered an insightful glimpse into the meticulous craft behind this celebrated beverage. Sweet vermouth, also referred to as red vermouth, is easily recognizable by its rich reddish-brown color, a visual cue to its indulgent nature. This variant stands out due to its significantly higher sugar content when compared to the dry vermouth counterparts.

Vodka

Traditionally rooted in Eastern Europe and the Nordic countries, vodka production has been a centuries-old practice primarily using fermented grains like wheat, rye, or corn, and sometimes potatoes or grapes, each imparting a distinct character to the spirit. The production process is meticulous, beginning with fermentation, when yeast converts sugars in the base ingredient to alcohol, followed by distillation to purify and increase alcohol content. Modern vodka often undergoes multiple distillations for purity and smoothness, followed by filtration, typically through charcoal, to eliminate impurities and achieve a neutral flavor profile. The critical role of water in diluting the vodka to the desired proof is acknowledged by distilleries, as it significantly influences the texture and taste. Finally, a resting period before bottling allows the flavors to blend and mellow, enhancing the vodka's smoothness.

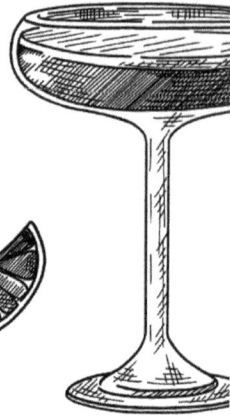

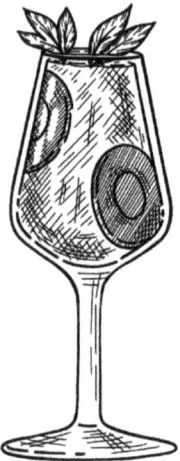

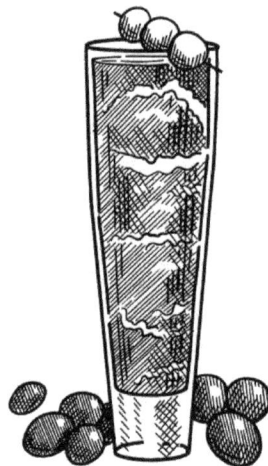

CODA

LAST CALL

Following the recognition and praise from the local food press and guests, we found ourselves courted by a number of property developers eager to see our concept take root in additional locales across Virginia, Maryland, and DC. These dialogues opened up intriguing possibilities for scaling our brand, enriching our team's expertise, and further evolving the Blend 111 experience.

In Loudoun County, we found a 5,000-square-foot expanse, with a private event space, something our patrons had requested often. Elsewhere, in the bustling center of Arlington's National Landing, a location emerged, poised at the forefront of a booming tech scene. Then there was Tysons Corner, with a spot directly across from a chic boutique hotel. Not to be outdone, the quaint charm of a historic building in Palisades beckoned, offering a fusion of tradition and modern style appealing to a wide range of clients. Each location presented its unique promise, weaving a rich mosaic of possibilities for Blend 111's ambitious expansion.

Anyone who has worked in the restaurant business will tell you that restaurants are hard—really hard. For every delighted guest, you have a broken air conditioner, a staff person who cannot make it to their shift, and a broken valve in your coffee machine that causes a flood at the bar. And that's all in one day. The margins are tiny and exist only when everything goes perfectly. At Blend 111, I worked at the bar, hosted, I had shifts as a server, dishwasher, and as the chef. I was the chief maintenance officer repairing, painting, and cleaning everything. During one ice storm, while cleaning the patio, I broke six ribs with a hard fall on the concrete.

In the summer of 2022, following the Town of Vienna's decision to terminate our outdoor patio, which constituted 50% of our seating, we had to downsize our remarkable staff to accommodate the reduced guest volume. Subsequently, our chef moved to Florida to be closer to his family. I had transitioned back into the IT consulting field earlier in the year. We cut back our operational hours, discontinuing lunch, brunch, and the Pescao pop-up on Mondays. While a dedicated portion of our staff pressed on, it was evident that much of the restaurant's original charm and zeal were fading. Concurrently, we grappled with inflation, which ate into our already slim margins. Every aspect, from ingredients to maintenance costs, saw substantial increases.

Given these hurdles, committing to another five years at Blend 111 felt very unwise. As the lease renewal loomed, I decided to sell the equipment, the remaining months on the lease, and the inventory. It was a difficult decision, but Blend 111 had run its course. In August 2023, the final dessert was served.

Despite the many challenges, the five-year odyssey of Blend 111 was a journey of enlightenment packed with lessons and growth. I left with a heart full of gratitude, treasuring the memories, regretting nothing, and overflowing with thanks for our dedicated staff and our tens of thousands of devoted guests who supported us throughout.

ABOUT THE AUTHOR

Michael Biddick is a seasoned technology entrepreneur recognized for founding and leading Fusion PPT as its CEO. Under his guidance, the company flourished, becoming a top-tier provider of cloud computing consulting and cybersecurity services. The firm won several "Best Places to Work" awards and recognition for quality. For nearly a decade, Fusion PPT achieved triple-digit growth and garnered acclaim for its strategic vision, market strategy, and project excellence, culminating in its sale in 2018.

Additionally, Biddick has made significant contributions to the media as a contributing editor at *InformationWeek* and *Network Computing* magazines. He has authored over 60 articles on cloud computing, federal CIO strategy, PMOs, and application performance enhancement. Biddick was a regular speaker at Interop for over a decade. His presentations there aided IT professionals worldwide in leveraging technology to enhance business operations.

As an author, Biddick has written multiple books that reflect his varied interests and knowledge. Biddick's *Federal Cloud Computing* provides a practical approach to implementing service-based IT in government, addressing policy, technology standards, and security issues. Additionally, he authored *43 Wine Regions*, a guide that blends his experiences as a sommelier with his tech expertise to delve into wine culture. This book garnered multiple accolades, including Gourmand's Best in the World and a Feathered Quill award. Biddick has also contributed to *Somm Journal*, *Food and Travel*, *FSR* and *Go World Travel* magazines.

In the culinary world, Biddick established and led Blend 111, an award-winning restaurant acclaimed for its organic and biodynamic wines, mirroring his passions for wine, coffee, and gourmet food. A skilled artisanal coffee roaster, Biddick holds certifications as a barista, Master of Bordeaux wine and French Wine Scholar (FSW) and was trained as a sommelier by the Court of Master Sommeliers. Blend 111 received significant recognition, including being named the third-best restaurant in the area by *Northern Virginia Magazine* and being featured in *The Washington Post*'s annual fall dining guide. The restaurant earned a RAMMY nomination and was named the Best Brunch in the Washington, DC, region by WTOP. During his tenure, Biddick appeared in several segments on Fox 5 *DC* and actively promoted sustainability at the restaurant, keynoting the NVCC Green Festival on their efforts.

Biddick's involvement extends into education and community service. He is the head debate coach at James Madison High School, nurturing students' argumentation skills for meaningful participation in democratic processes. He holds the title of National Speech and Debate Association's Donus D. Roberts coach, with his team consistently ranking among the nation's top 100 and regularly sending members to national tournaments. He also founded and leads the Sharon Sharko Debate Foundation, a nonprofit dedicated to advancing high school debate and speech programs since 2017.

Biddick holds dual Bachelor of Arts degrees in Political Science and African American Studies from the University of Wisconsin-Madison and a Master of Science in Information Systems and Telecommunications from Johns Hopkins University. He resides in Vienna, VA, and is conversant in French, Italian, and Spanish.

INDEX

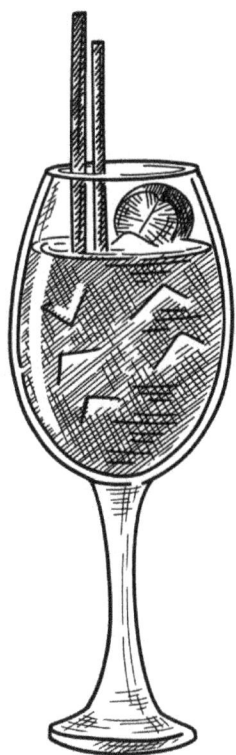

www.ingramcontent.com/pod-product-compliance
Lightning Source LLC
Chambersburg PA
CBHW040410110426
42812CB00012B/2513